Synopsis and Overview
of Lone Women

DAMON GREENE

TABLE OF CONTENTS

CHAPTER 1

The people, the narrative, and the twists are amazing!
The start catches you in! The tension continues rising! It
was impossible to convey the dark and tormented
individuals so well!

Each of them battles their inner demons. They are far
from ideal and have flaws. You may relate to them
readily because of this.
Typically, I don't like historical fiction. Yet, this work
offers us a wonderful synthesis of many genres,
including fantasy, women's literature, historical fiction,
and horror. This stirring tale of feminism and monster
survival is set in Montana in the early 20th century.
This book offers us a fantastic blend of several genres,
including fantasy, women's literature, historical fiction,
and horror. This stirring tale of feminism and monster
survival is set in Montana in the early 20th century.

Adelaide Henry is a strange, unusual, powerful, tall, and
confined lady. Raised more like a mule than a person,
she decided to control her destiny at the age of 31. The
day she set her Redondo farmhouse on fire, destroying
the remains of her parents Glenville and Eleanor Henry,
her life was forever altered.

Moving to Montana to start over, she hauled her luggage that contained a special delivery, her great secret, and her curse. There, destiny brought her together with the suspicious mother and her four blind boys.

She works hard to keep her secret a secret, both for the benefit of herself and the townies. What if, though, she is not the only cursed person in this town? The town already has rotted from hypocrisy, injustice, and greed. What if she is not the only single woman in the community battling the demons that hide behind human fur? Doesn't she need to do something to survive?

LBGTQIA subgenre/themes the female experience, strong women, outsiders & outcasts, companionship, community, homesteading, secrets from the family, loneliness, and representation
Writing Style: Three parts, quick pacing, character-driven, and different points of view.
The summary does a great job of preserving readers' reading interests while describing this as the tale of a lady who is forced to leave her home, and her history, and start again. Just certain family secrets cannot be kept private, which is the issue.

My reading experience: Holy crap, this is a funny, surprising tale. Victor LaValle deserves a lot of respect for the brief chapters that kept the action moving quickly. As I type this, I'm seeing how many narratives LaValle was able to include in this larger narrative. Adelaide

Henry, the main character, is the main focus, and all the side stories revolve around her. However, LaValle does a fantastic job of incorporating fresh characters into her journey to create multiple central figures to root for. They are all fascinating, complex, and strong women, hence the title Lone Women. The historical backdrop of this tale is one of my favorites. The initial setup, in which Adelaide sets off on her own to homestead in Montana, was fascinating. I liked reading about every step she took to get there and how terrifying it would have been for me. Being alone in a foreign environment with unfamiliar noises and no one to share the burden as you spend the night in a dark building with no power. It felt authentic to me.

The suspense is heightened by Adelaide's steamer trunk. Man, I've never been that enquiring and eager for information!
There was a tendency for me to become frustrated as new characters enter and exit the story, particularly in Part II. This occurs to me sometimes when I prefer an established narrative to one that has just been presented, but in Part III, all of the subplots are crucial to getting us there.

In the early 1900s, when the United States was still being settled, there was a process known as "homesteading," in which if you could live on a plot of land and make it prosperous and productive after three years, it would become yours.

Adelaide Henry is fleeing her childhood home in search of a piece of land in Montana while carrying only a steamer trunk to protect her from the fire she started and the horrors within. Adelaide is hesitant to let the trunk leave her sight, even though it is securely closed with a strong padlock. She's going to attempt to lay a claim as a "lone woman" in a state that permits it. Yet Adelaide is quite different from everyone else who has settled in Montana, just as Montana is very different from California.

Adelaide is hiding a terrible secret. one who kills everyone in her vicinity. Sometimes the devil you know won't let you go, and family history and secrets hang around your neck like heavy chains. Victor Lavalle has crafted a dramatic, atmospheric, historical romp through the colonization adventure in the early 1900s, but he has twisted his story with terrifying imagery and terrifying situations with demons you won't expect.
Readers of many genres will enjoy this fast-paced, impossible-to-put-down adventure that will take you through turns and spine-tingling moments.
Adelaide Henry had been a farmer on Tuesday. Since Wednesday, she has been on the run.

I had the luxury of going into the narrative blind since I had the opportunity to read this book early. I'll attempt to extend the same courtesy to you by praising this book without giving too much away about its narrative.

The year is 1914, and a 31-year-old Black lady named Adelaide Henry has moved from her family's property in California to a homestead in Montana. The novel begins with a horrifying sight of devastation, and our protagonist is fleeing all she knows to get away from her past. • Lone Woman surpassed so many of my expectations! She carries a big trunk that she must defend at all times because once it's opened, everyone around her appears to vanish.

I was eager to take this book back up after a hard day at work because I disliked having to put it down. It combines many genres—horror, historical fiction, and western—and is a superb illustration of author Victor Lavalle's skill at crafting compelling narratives. I think this could be my new favorite book of his (January seems to be my month for 5-star books!) The narrative twists are many, the novel goes rapidly, and we get to see the tale from many different characters' points of view. If you're still not persuaded, take up this novel only to cheer for a Black lady who is seeking forgiveness and is determined to make it through the arid northwest wilderness of early 20th-century America.

LONE WOMAN begins with an explosive chapter (one of my Fave openers to a book ever) and then moves on to shorter, more rapid-fire chapters. Adelaid Henry, our protagonist, is escaping the West while carrying a sinister secret. The narrative, which takes place in the 1910s, is very engrossing in terms of both atmosphere and concepts. You'll lose track of the fact that it's 2023 since the author made such a great job of establishing this for the audience. As the suspense in this book will be twisting and disturbing, it's best not to read too many reviews before starting it. When Adelaide travels to the West and meets many new people who become a part of her life, she is concerned that the secret she is keeping in her steamer trunk may ultimately cause everything to fall apart.

The fact that Adelaide is in danger coming from all sides is one of the reasons this novel works so effectively. She is not fully prepared for it after living on a warm California farm where she had the support of her parents and a community. There is also the enormous achievement of just existing. Then there is the issue of a woman surviving alone. Every knock on the door may be the last one you hear since you are miles away from any help and no one can see you or hear you.

Every new person you meet has the potential to become a friend or be planning to rob you. Despite Adelaide's strength and vigilance, she is limited in what she can do because of the burden of keeping her secret.
LaValle is not satisfied to have one storyline dominate the others in this situation. Instead, as Adelaide's circumstances change, everyone struggles for a place, and the novel changes from being one thing to another. The finest horror books, in my opinion, are those in which you never predict what will occur next, and this was virtually always the case in this book.

This novel, in contrast to other fiction of the era, recognizes (and focuses) the presence of underprivileged individuals. Even in a culture like this, where one might experience more acceptance than they could elsewhere, that acceptance is always dependent on convenience. I was pleased to see LGBT people in this novel, however, I should point out that it does include misgendering (which is to be expected given the period). This does an excellent job of developing a more comprehensive, more honest perspective of a historical place and period, however, there was one part where I had a few observations.

Very varied characters, superb writing, and one of the most memorable storylines I've ever read. I opened this book with no prior knowledge other than the title. Going into this novel with as little knowledge as you can allows you to fully immerse yourself in the mystery and mayhem of Lone Women. Did Adelaide and Elizabeth's parents act cruelly in the situation? The issue of "what would I do?" arises as the tale unfolds and we go into the odd mind of Victor LaValle.

And believe me when I say that this wonderful, yes great book is powered by this thought! And when we encounter a family that coped with comparable conditions but used a very different strategy, our internal dialogue becomes louder, and we may have modified our first response to the crucial issue.

You won't be able to put this book down until the very end since it is such a crazy and terrifying story that is handled with such skill. The finest literature I've read this year, without a doubt, belongs to Victor LaValle.

CHAPTER 2

EXCERPT

In this world, there are two types of people: those who endure humiliation and those who pass away as a result. Adelaide Henry might have identified as the former on Tuesday, but by Wednesday she wasn't so sure. Why would she stroll through her family's farmhouse carrying an Atlas jar of gasoline, dump that gasoline over the kitchen floor, and the dining room table, and soak the sofa in the den if she was only trying to survive?

After emptying the first Atlas jar, she wondered why she should return to the kitchen for the second one before climbing the stairs to the second story and hearing the splash of gasoline with each step. Was she attempting to die or was she trying to live? In the Lucerne Valley of California, there were 27 African farmer households in 1915. These included Adelaide and her parents. There would be only 26 after today. Adelaide made it to the landing on the second level. She scarcely noticed the gasoline scent anymore. Fresh cuts covered her hands, yet she was pain-free. Her bedroom and her parent's bedroom were both located on the second level.

The allure of property in this valley convinced Adelaide's parents to move there from the east. Americans were urged by the federal government to settle in California. The local inhabitants had been wiped off and evicted from the area. It was now time to part with everything. The African Society issued a request to "colonize" Southern California after 1866, and this offer was one of the few that the US gave to even its Black residents.

Hundreds of people showed up there, including the Henrys. In Arkansas, they were not going to have a fair chance, there was no doubt about that. Homesteading is what the federal government refers to as. To feed their cattle, Glenville and Eleanor Henry emigrated to California where they raised alfalfa and wild grass. Glenville researched Luther Burbank's writings, and in 1908 they started cultivating the botanist's Santa Rosa plums. The apple tasted sweet and independent to Adelaide. Since she was twelve years old, Adelaide has assisted her father in working the fields and orchards. worked much longer with her mother in the barn and the kitchen. 31 years of life spent on this property.
Thirty-one.

She would immediately set it all on fire.

"Ma'am?"

The wagon man's voice surprised Adelaide.
Oh my God, what is that odor?
He was at the front door, with little more than a screen
door separating him from the inside. Adelaide was
standing on the second floor, near the doorway of her
parent's room. She shook the half-full Atlas jar in her
hand. After turning, she yelled to the landing.
I'll be leaving in five, Mr. Cole.
She heard him even if she couldn't see him. A scarcely
heard elderly Black man's grumble that nevertheless
manages to be as loud as a thunderclap. She was
reminded of her father by it.

You mentioned that only five minutes ago, right?
Adelaide could hear the screen door's springs
squeaking. She saw a vision of Mr. Cole approaching
the bottom of the steps, and Adelaide spilling the last of
the gasoline directly over his head. She also saw
Adelaide reaching into her pocket for a match, lighting it,
and dropping it directly upon Mr. Cole. Combustion
follows.

She called out to him instead since she didn't want to
murder the elderly guy.
Have you yet loaded my trunk onto the wagon? she
yelled.
Quite quiet.
The screen door finally opened and sighed. He wasn't
inside yet. On the porch, he shouted to her once again.

He said, "I tried. Yet, that object weighs more than my dreadful horse. What did you bring in there? My whole existence," she reflected. anything remains important.

She called down again after turning to face her parents' bedroom door.
I'll give you five, Mr. Cole. Together, we'll load the trunk onto the wagon.

He grumbled again, but this time he didn't swear at her, and she didn't hear the sound of his wagon's wheels squealing as it left. It was as near to an "okay" as she was going to get from a guy like Mr. Cole.
Would she have truly set him ablaze? She was speechless. Yet what individuals will do in times of need is astonishing.

Adelaide Henry opened the door to her parent's bedroom by turning the handle, entered, closed the door behind her, and then stood in the dark and in quiet. The thick drapes were drawn closed. Around daybreak, she had completed it. Once she had brought Glenville and Eleanor's corpses inside and put them to sleep.

Now, they were lying in bed together. the same location as Adelaide's conception. She had draped a sheet over their bodies, so they were merely shapes. Their blood had permeated everything. Red shadows of their bodies could be seen.

She walked over to her dad's side. When the blood
dried, the garment clung to his skin. The sheet had been
raised over his head by her. It is preferable. She was
unwilling to see what was still left of him. From his
forehead to his feet, she drenched his body with
gasoline.
Adelaide has now shifted to her mother's side.
To conceal the harm done to Eleanor's neck, she had
only pulled the covers up to her chin on her side. She
had struggled to completely cover her mother with the
cloth.

It seems strange to be uncomfortable about that section
given all the other harm done to Eleanor's body.
Adelaide tried to pour the remainder of the gasoline out
while tilting the jar over her mother's head, but she was
unsuccessful. Her mother's eyes were wide and vacant
as she held them over Eleanor.

She was unable to force herself to carry it out. She
placed the jug on the floor and knelt near the bed. She
spoke softly into Eleanor's lifeless ear.
Adelaide remarked, "You kept too many secrets. See
how much it cost you,
After saying that, she stood up and grabbed for her
pocket. The silhouette of a Black man operating a plow
was the matchbox's representation of the African
Society's emblem. She lit a match and then saw it burn.
She threw it towards the bed, where her father was hit
by it.

She hurriedly turned to avoid having to see the corpses being caught, but she heard it. As though everyone in the space inhaled deeply all at once. She felt heat spread over her scalp and neck a split second later, but as she left the room, the flames were still licking at her flesh. She realized that guilt, not the fire, had been the source of her pain.

Her right knee gave out while she was standing on the upstairs landing, and she almost fell. kneeling and placing one hand on the handrail. That was her doing. The door had her parents on fire. She may perhaps remain with them. She gave it some thought. It wouldn't take long for her to catch fire since there was enough gasoline on her hands and clothes. Return to the bedroom, kneel at the foot of their bed and prepare to be absorbed. A familial line should end. She deserved to get that. What sort of daughter would act in the manner that she has during the last 24 hours? A filthy, awful daughter.

Adelaide soon rose to her feet, hardly realizing she had done so. It was as though her body desired survival even though her spirit did not. She stood up and moved ahead. next, after that. It thought she was about to go. Even as she gripped the railing and ascended the steps, she questioned who made that decision.
She emerged from the screen door and Mr. Cole exclaimed, "Oh, there you are. From her, he turned to face the house. Has he yet detected smoke? Could he hear the crackling of the walls in the upper bedroom?

His buckboard wagon was parked by the porch; the horse was almost as underweight as the driver. Mr. Cole was six inches taller than Adelaide, who was forty pounds heavier. He couldn't raise the trunk, which makes sense.

The Seward steamer trunk has grips on both sides. Mr. Cole took one end, while Adelaide took the other. She lifted while bending her legs. Mr. Cole puffed under the pressure.

Now hurry up, he urged. He wasn't doing much work, but he still enjoyed giving orders.

Mr. Cole tugged along as she pulled the trunk in the direction of the wagon's bed.

As they got to the wagon, they made one final attempt to place it in the bed. The four wooden wheels of the wagon creaked as it fell a few inches. Mr. Cole's horse moved forward as though attempting to escape the weight. Mr. Cole and Adelaide both felt out of breath as they straightened up.

When she entered the wagon, Adelaide. Other than that trunk, she had only packed her travel bag. Everything had already been packed and was waiting inside the doorway. On the spring seat next to her, Mr. Cole seated himself.

CONCLUSION

Go slower, go slower, you are coming close to the finish, I had to tell you at one point, but I was unable to slow down. I needed a fantastic horror novel, and as always LaValle delivers. The characters are just so fantastic. The prose is poetic. The flow is excellent. The environment is ideal (Montana in the 1900s). The conclusion is also. I have nothing to complain about. But, I would caution readers that since this is a horror book, there is some blood and other graphic details that can make some readers queasy.

"Lone Women" follows Adelaide Henry, a 31-year-old woman. Adelaide seemed to be evading something. She departs with nothing more than a travel bag and a steamer trunk, leaving behind her family farm and the secrets it contains. She decides to move from California to Montana because she has previously read newspaper clippings about how a single woman can end up settling and acquiring land in that state. She also hopes it's far enough away to keep her secrets a secret. Naturally, things don't go as planned, and Adelaide is forced to choose between telling her new friends the truth about her family and continuing to flee. Adelaide did well. I felt bad for her. A woman in her 30s was forced to live with her parents because of a sinister secret. A Black woman in America in 1914, known in the novel as a "Negro," has few alternatives, but she is determined to continue, even if part of her questions why she is continuing.

She demonstrates how strong she is by going by ship to Seattle and then by rail to Montana. The other people we encounter, such as Bertie Brown, Fiona, Grace, and her son Sam, are great. I wanted a little novella on Bertie and Fiona's romance since I adored them. While the secrets that Grace and Sam revealed to Adelaide and she came as a surprise, it is obvious that this is why they were pulled to Adelaide and them. The fact that LaValle can fully develop each character in a little over 200 pages still astounds me.

There is no word wasted. We also meet a few other people, such as the Mudges and eventually the Reeds, about whom you begin to be concerned once they discover Adelaide's secret. Fantastic writing was used. The reason it sometimes seems repeated is that Adelaide is still troubled by the things her mother said and didn't say to her. Her mother's spirit sometimes follows her as she goes. Throughout this era, Montana was in a desolate environment. You have the impression that anything may kill you. You can also see how many people rushed to the Reeds' and their alleged charity.

Yet there are always conditions attached to generosity. Moreover, I thought it was fantastic that LaValle could teach Adelaide how to act differently in Montana since she is Black. Even though she eventually encounters only white individuals. Her "relationship" in the novel caught me off guard a little since I wasn't sure how people would have reacted to it then. But, it didn't matter in the end.

It's difficult to discuss this one without giving anything away, but if you're even somewhat fascinated by the concept of a horror/western story about a lady fleeing her past while toting an enigmatic steamer trunk. A trunk that, when opened, often causes fatalities...

Alternatively, you should read Lone Women if you appreciate the notion of a book that focuses on women and utilizes horror to beautifully nuanced address problems like racism, sexism, and homophobia. The mining boom has ended, abandoned ghost towns dot the landscape, and it's the Wild, Wild West in early 20th-century America.

These are desperate times for desperate people. Adelaide encounters all kinds of people, each with a tale that reflects the founding of America. At different moments, she is both befriended and deceived by both likable and hateful individuals. The relationship she develops with other single, independent women who are born underprivileged and often shunned for no reason at all is the book's greatest strength (i.e. based on their sex, physical build, sexual orientation, race, socio-economic status, refusal to marry, etc.). women who are committed to surviving in a difficult environment and a harsher society. Women who are forced to downplay their abilities, swallow their pride, control their emotions, and repress their anger voluntarily submit to the laws of the land and societal mores that were developed as a result of racism, sexism, and other forms of discrimination.

The themes of redemption, forgiveness, and tenacity are explored in this work. Adelaide's narrative, which is beset on all sides, will keep the reader wondering while also making their hearts pound and their hands sweat.

A thrilling experience for fans of westerns, horror, and those looking for a well-planned novel in the genre.